How To Draw
Flowers
For Kids & Beginners

greenthumbpublishing@gmail.com

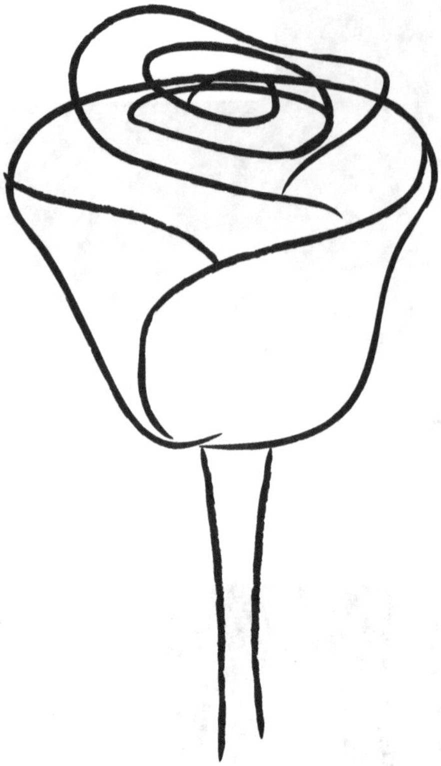

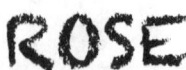

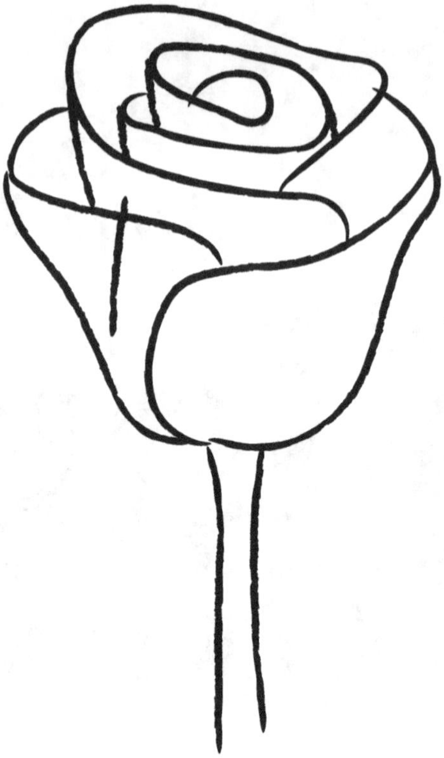

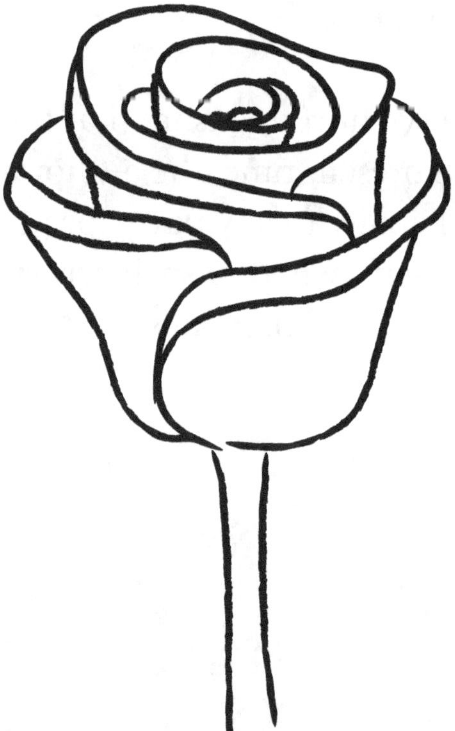

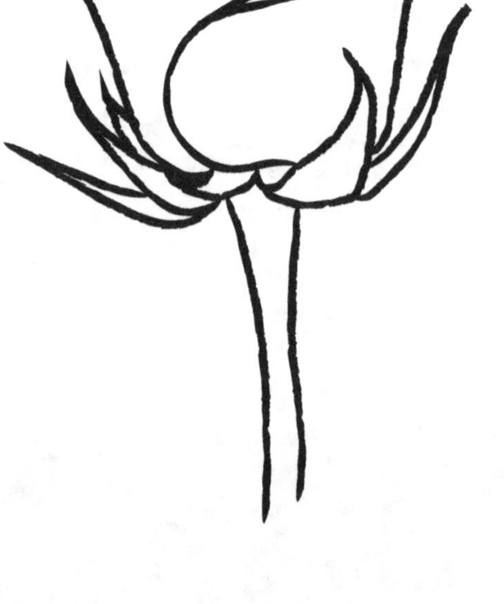

PRACTICE HERE!

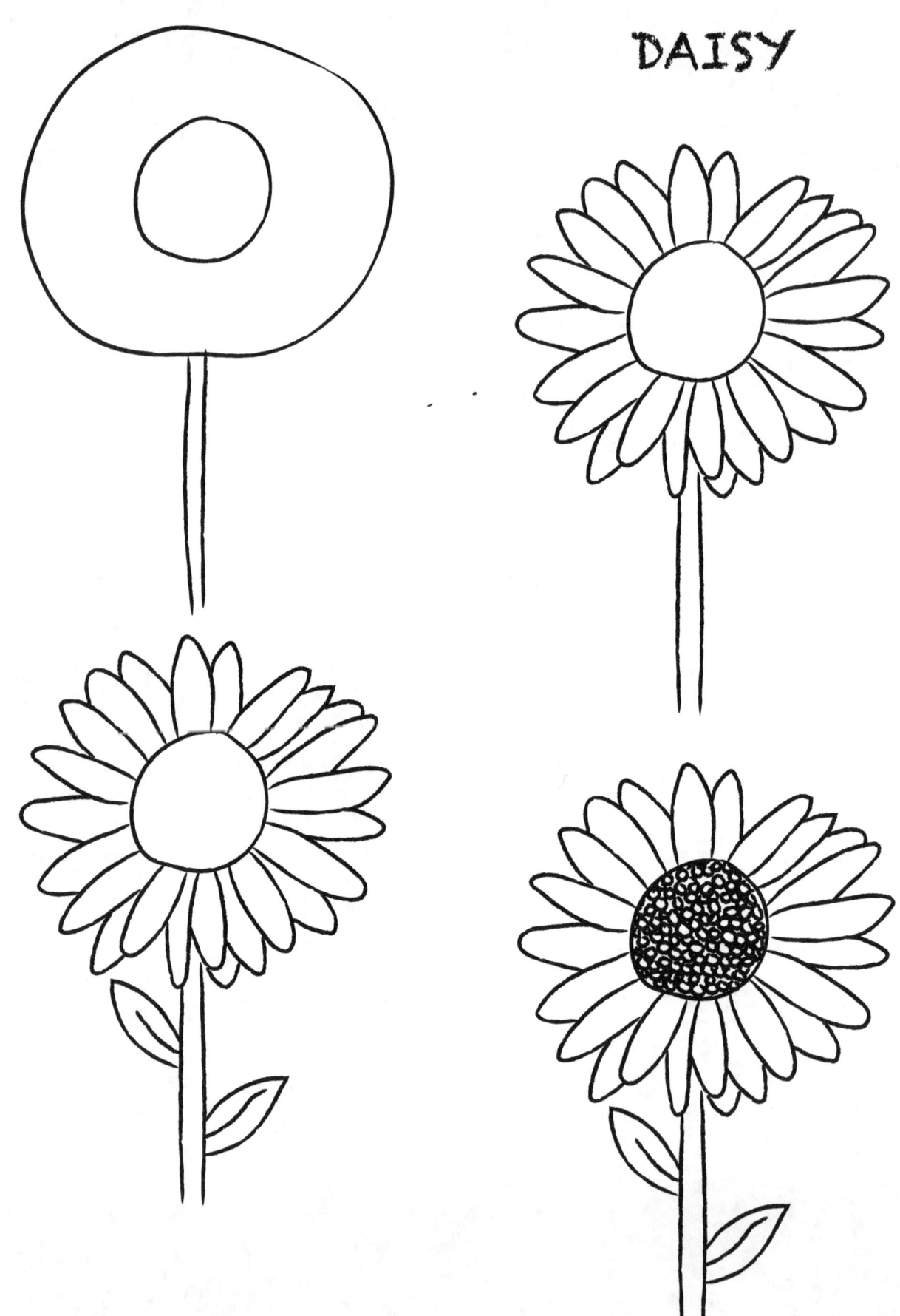

DAISY

PRACTICE HERE!

TULIP

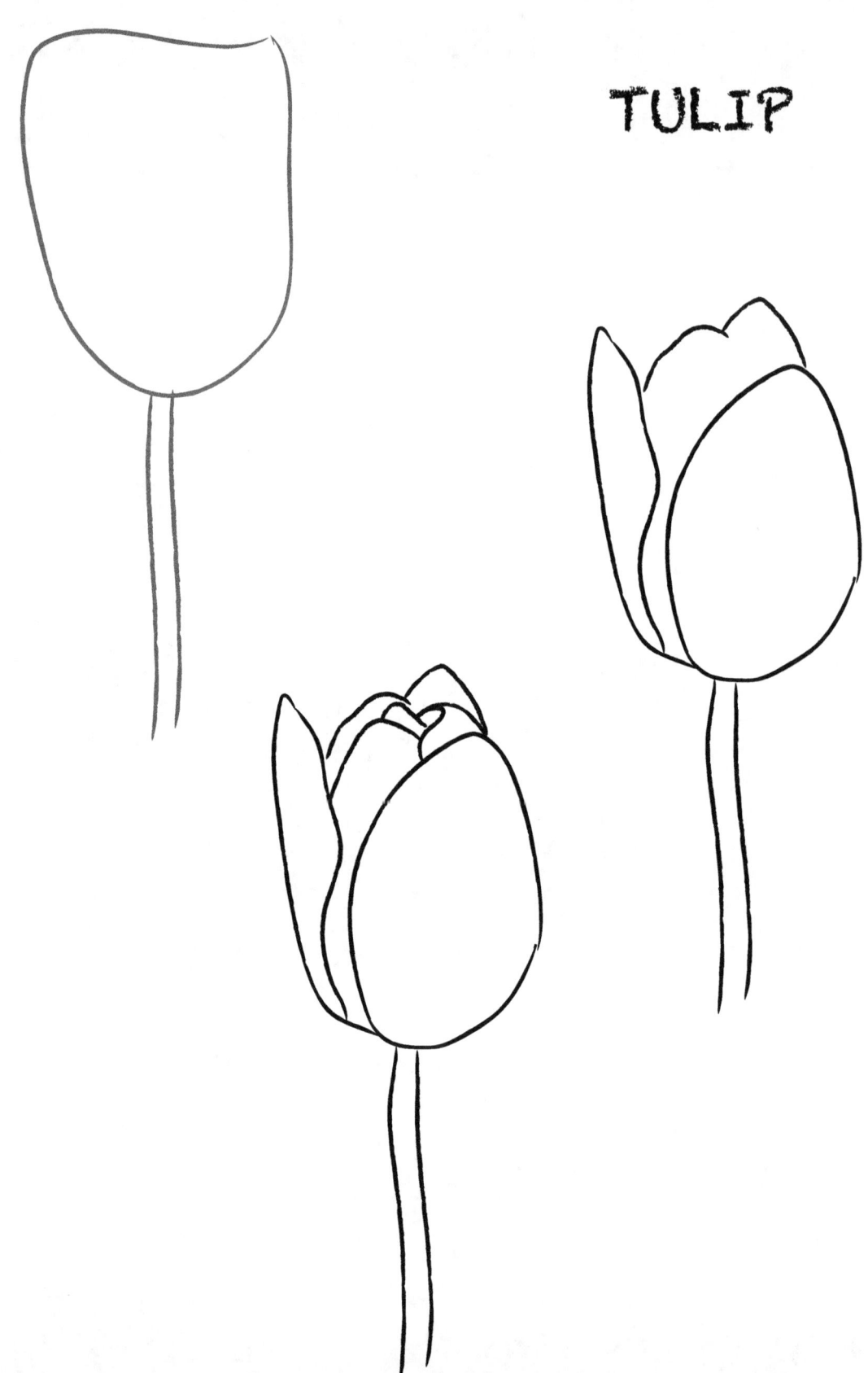

PRACTICE HERE!

DAFFODIL

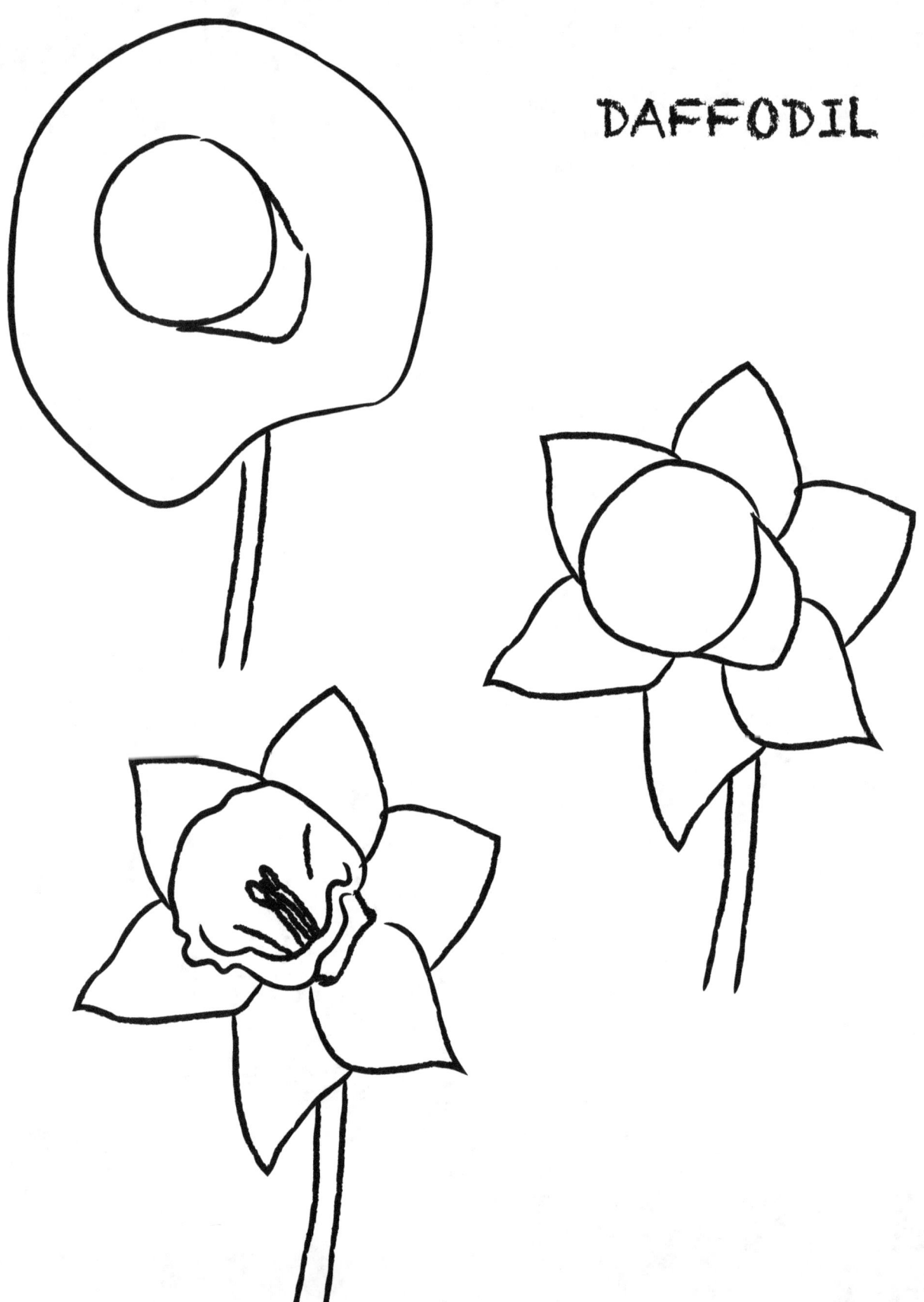

PRACTICE HERE!

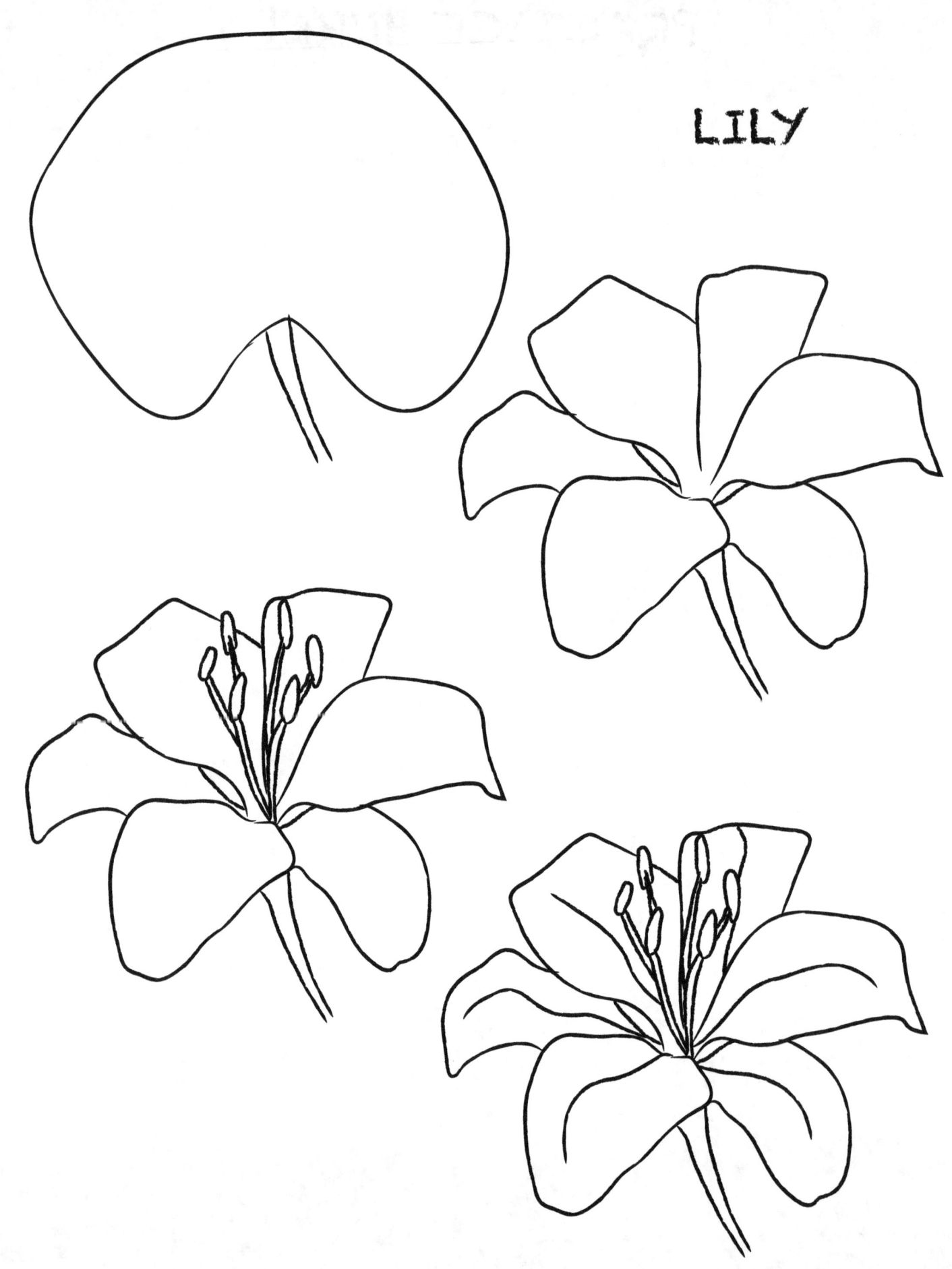

LILY

PRACTICE HERE!

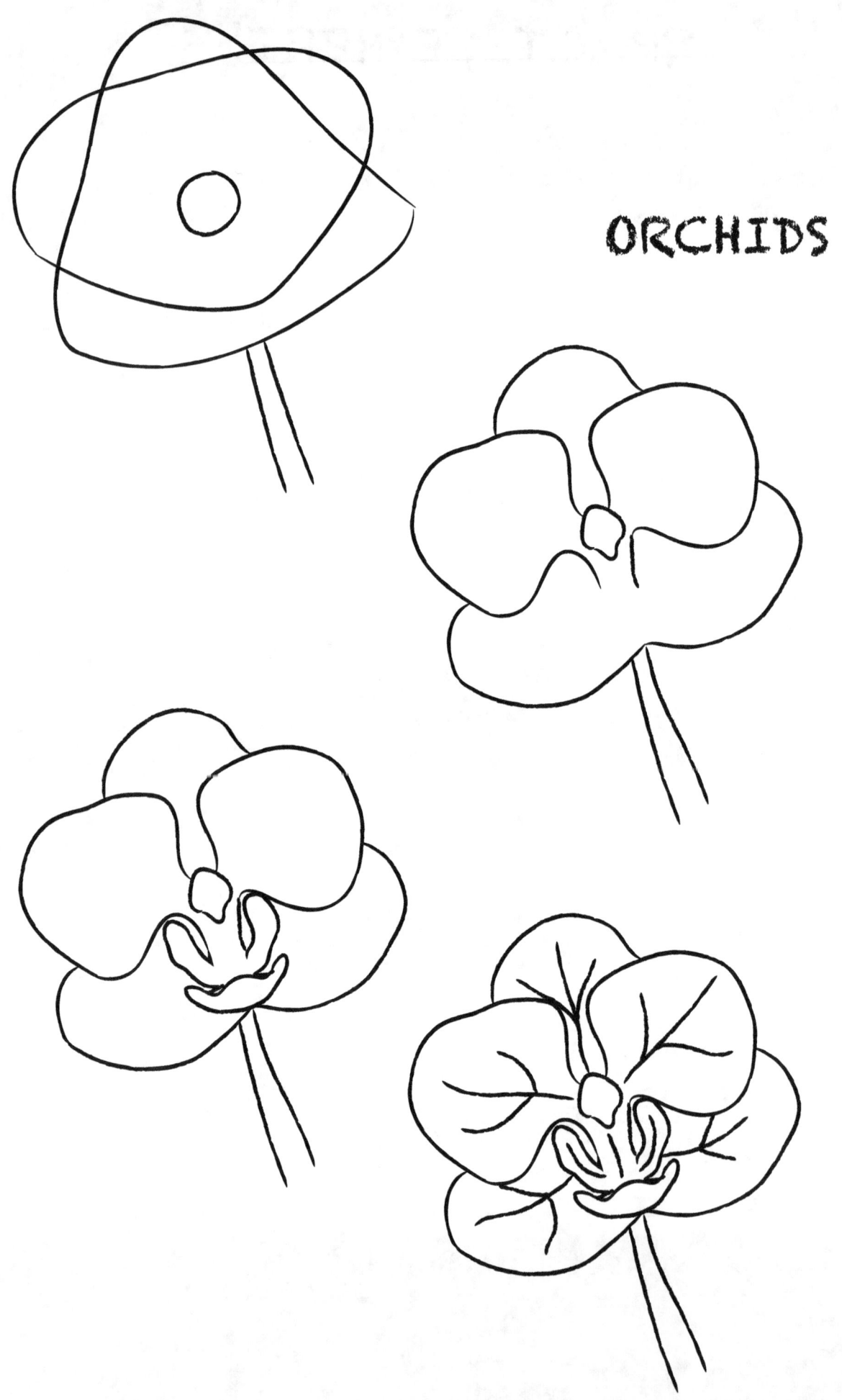

ORCHIDS

PRACTICE HERE!

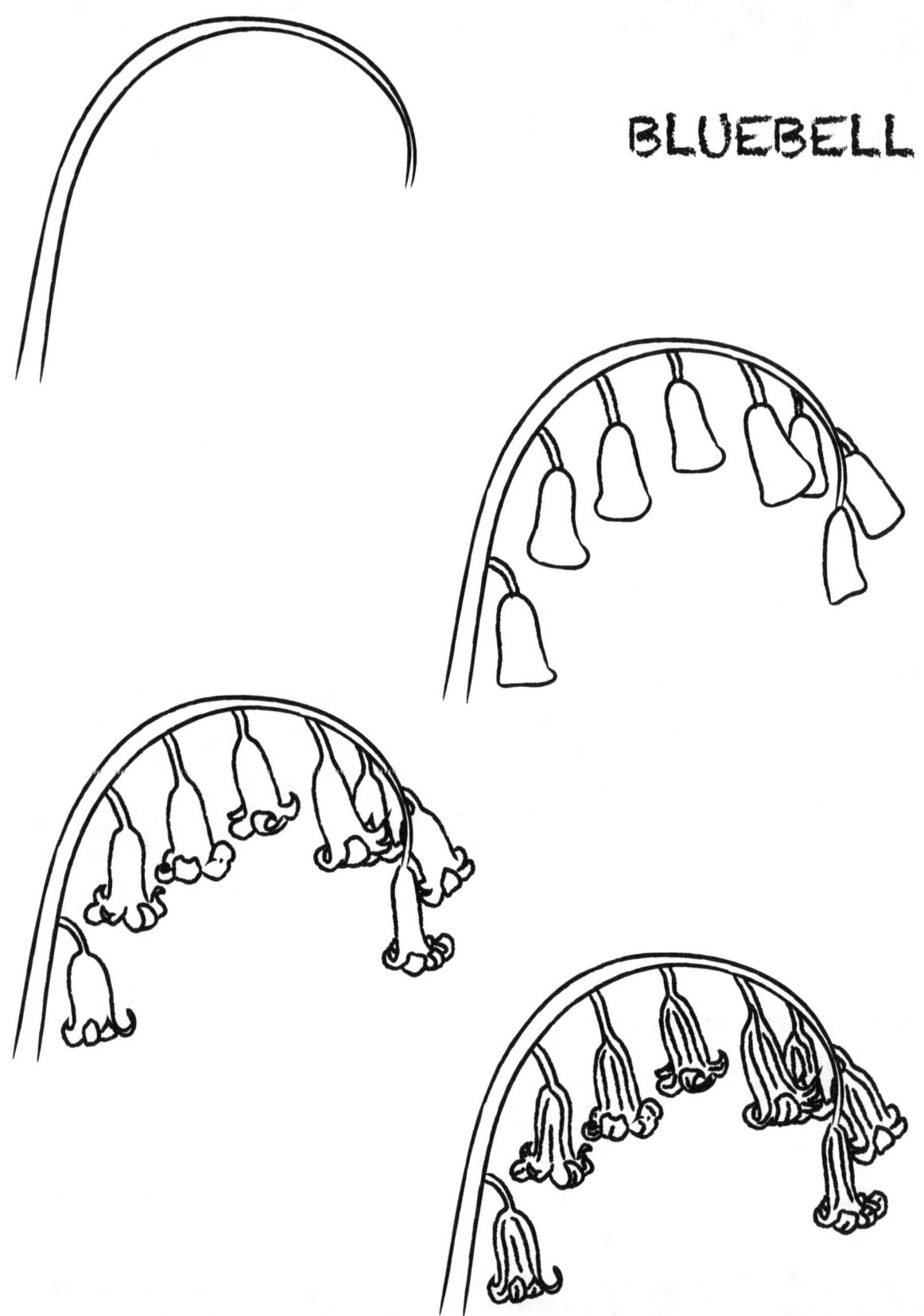

BLUEBELL

PRACTICE HERE!

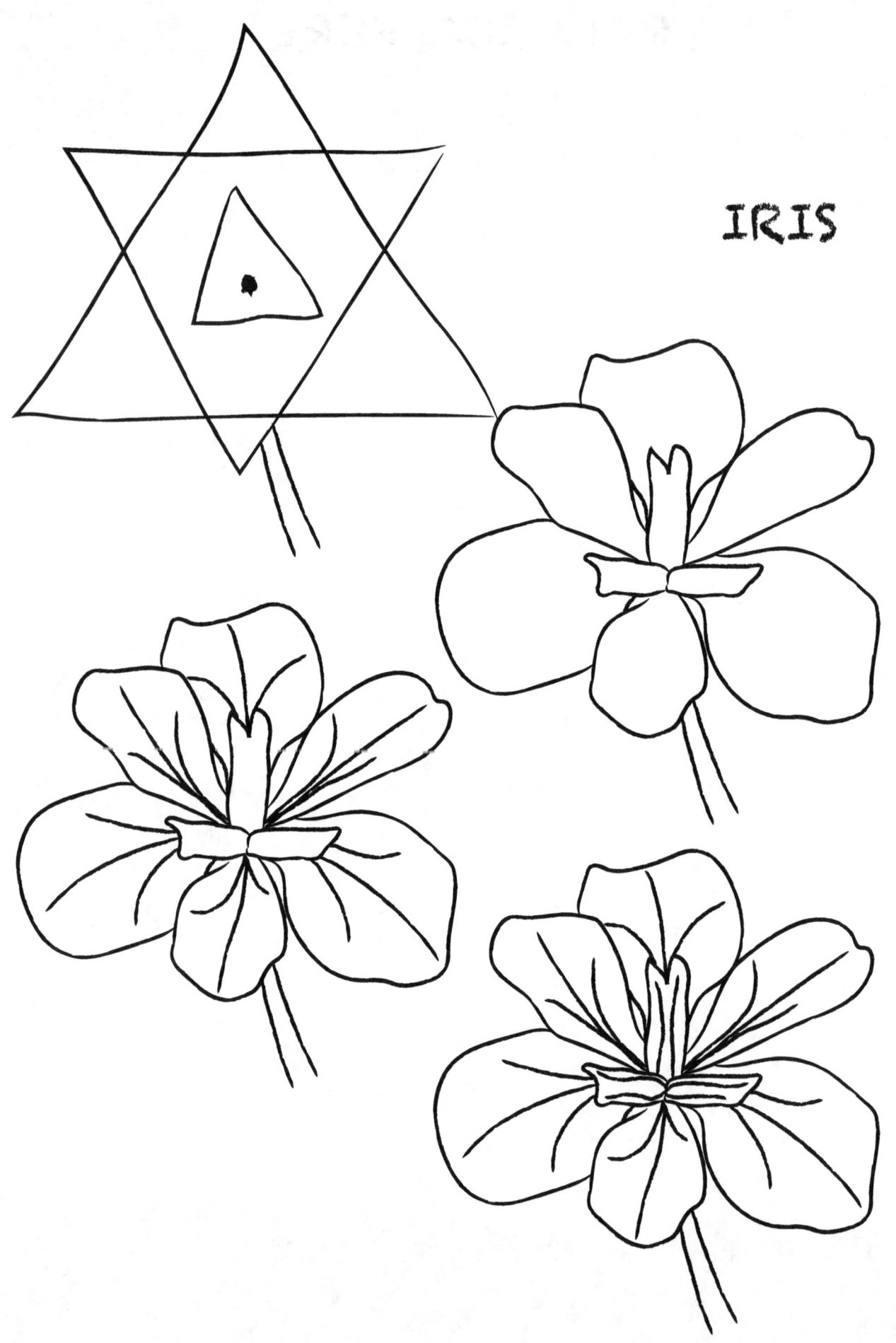

IRIS

PRACTICE HERE!

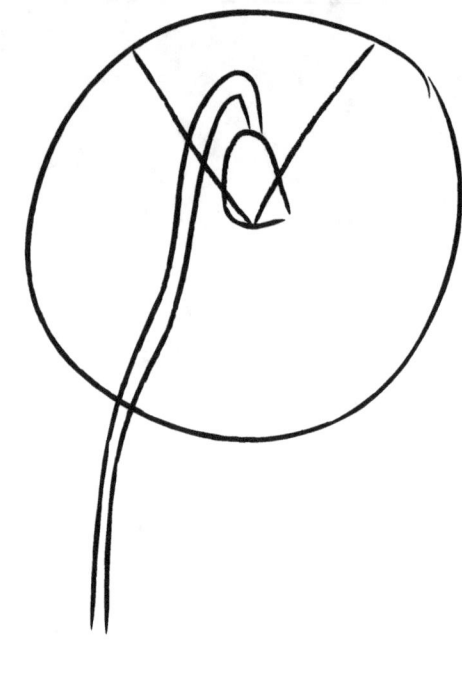

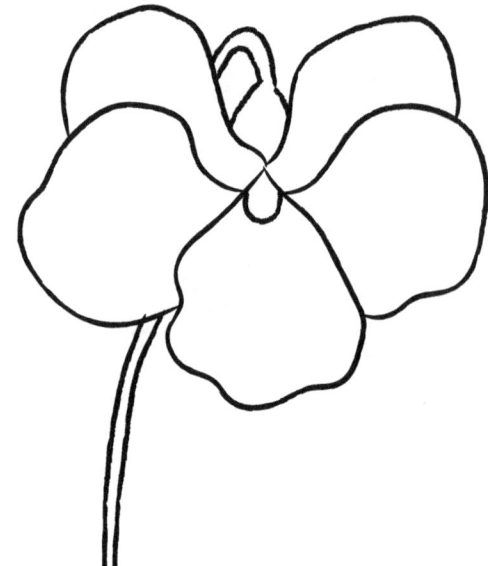

VIOLET

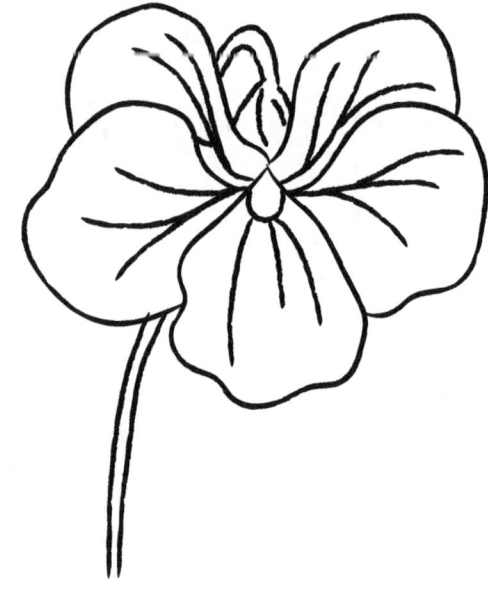

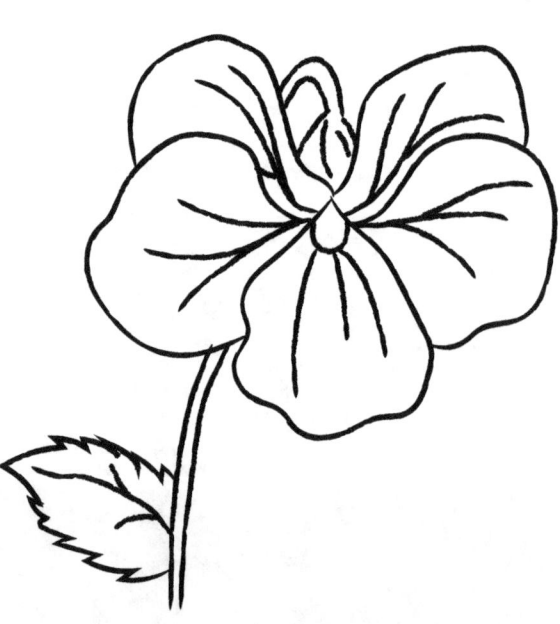

PRACTICE HERE!

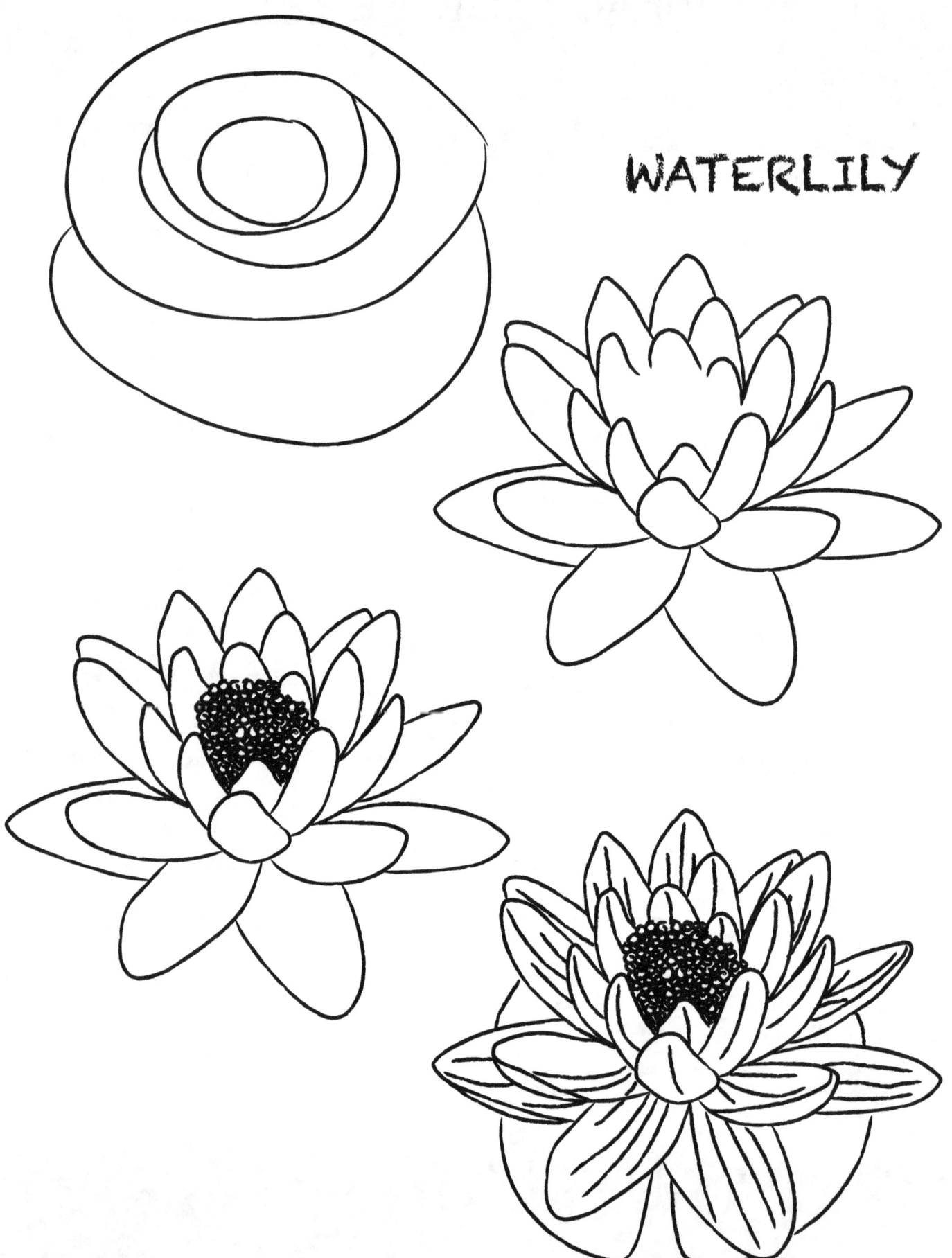

WATERLILY

PRACTICE HERE!

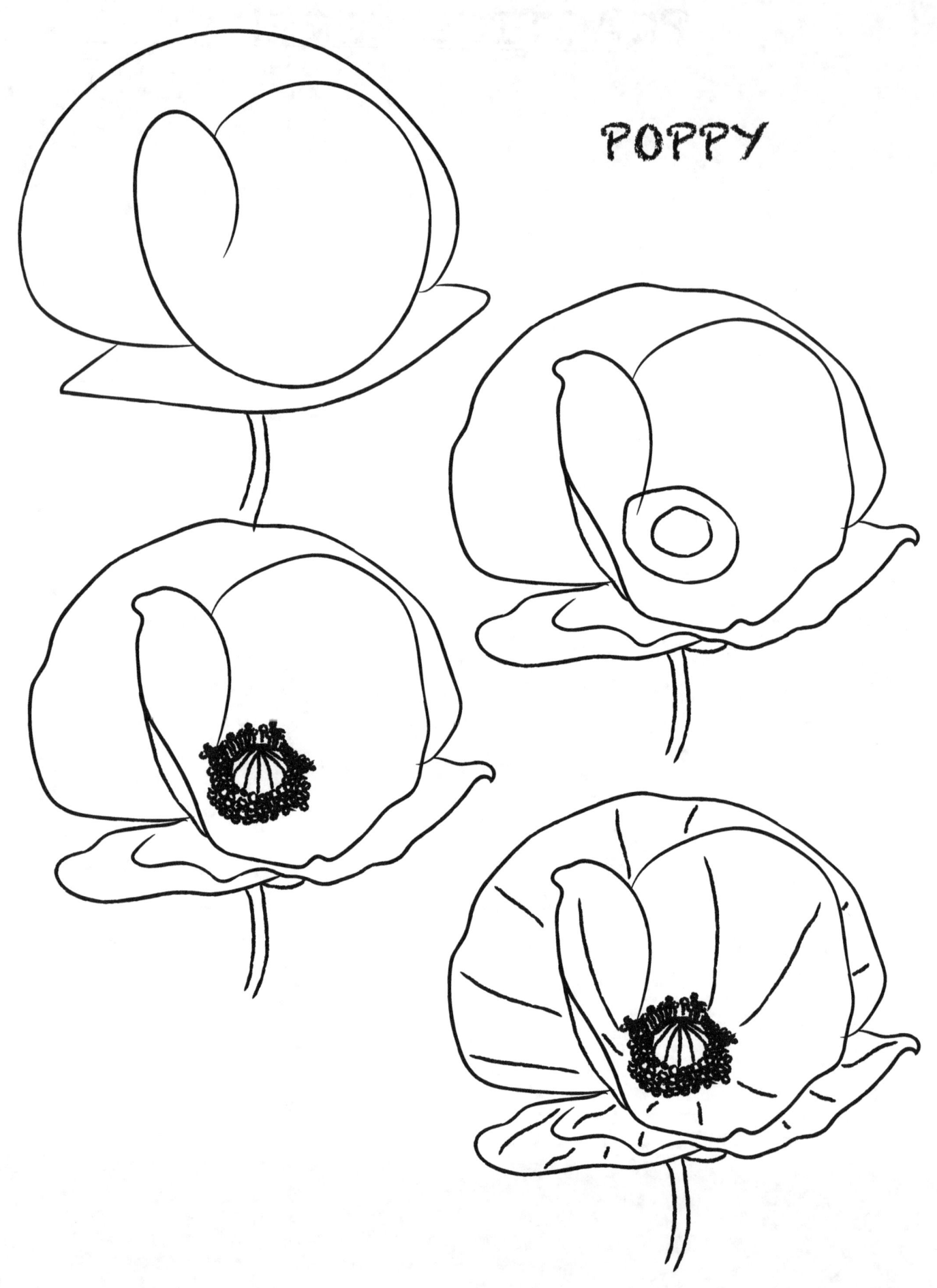

POPPY

PRACTICE HERE!

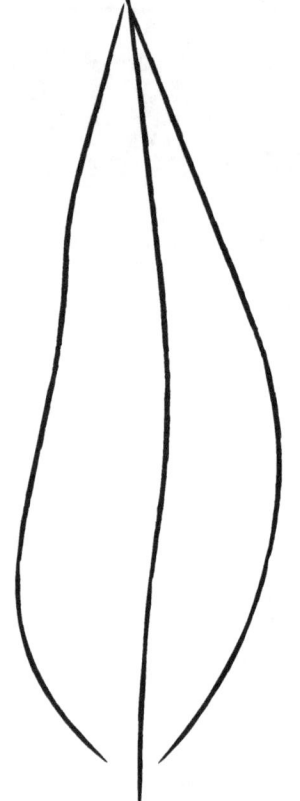

FOXGLOVE

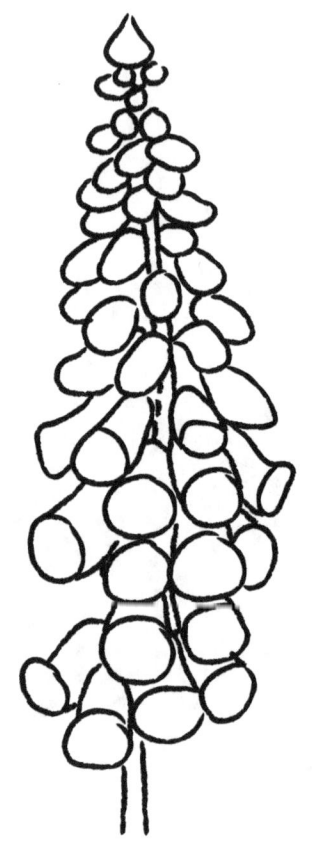

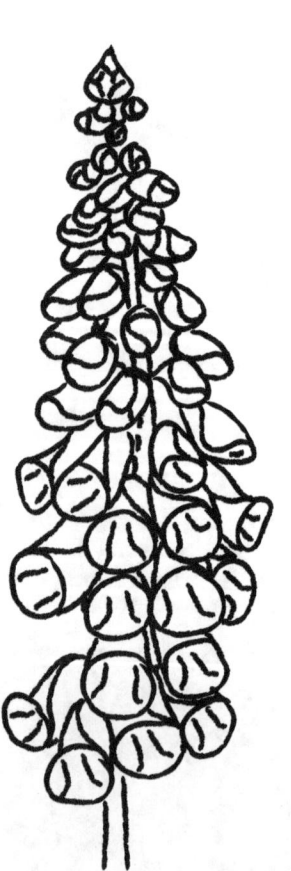

PRACTICE HERE!

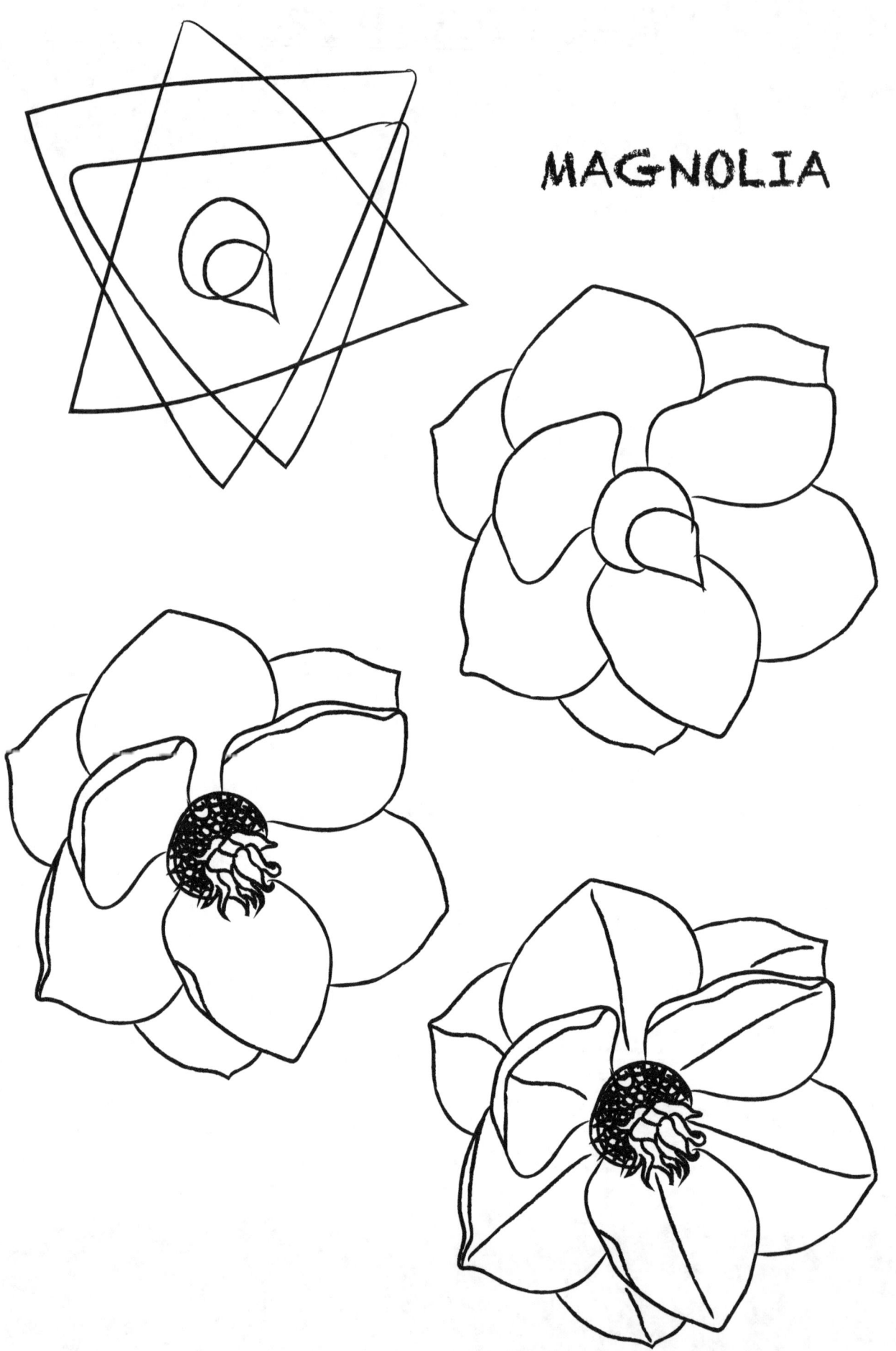

MAGNOLIA

PRACTICE HERE!

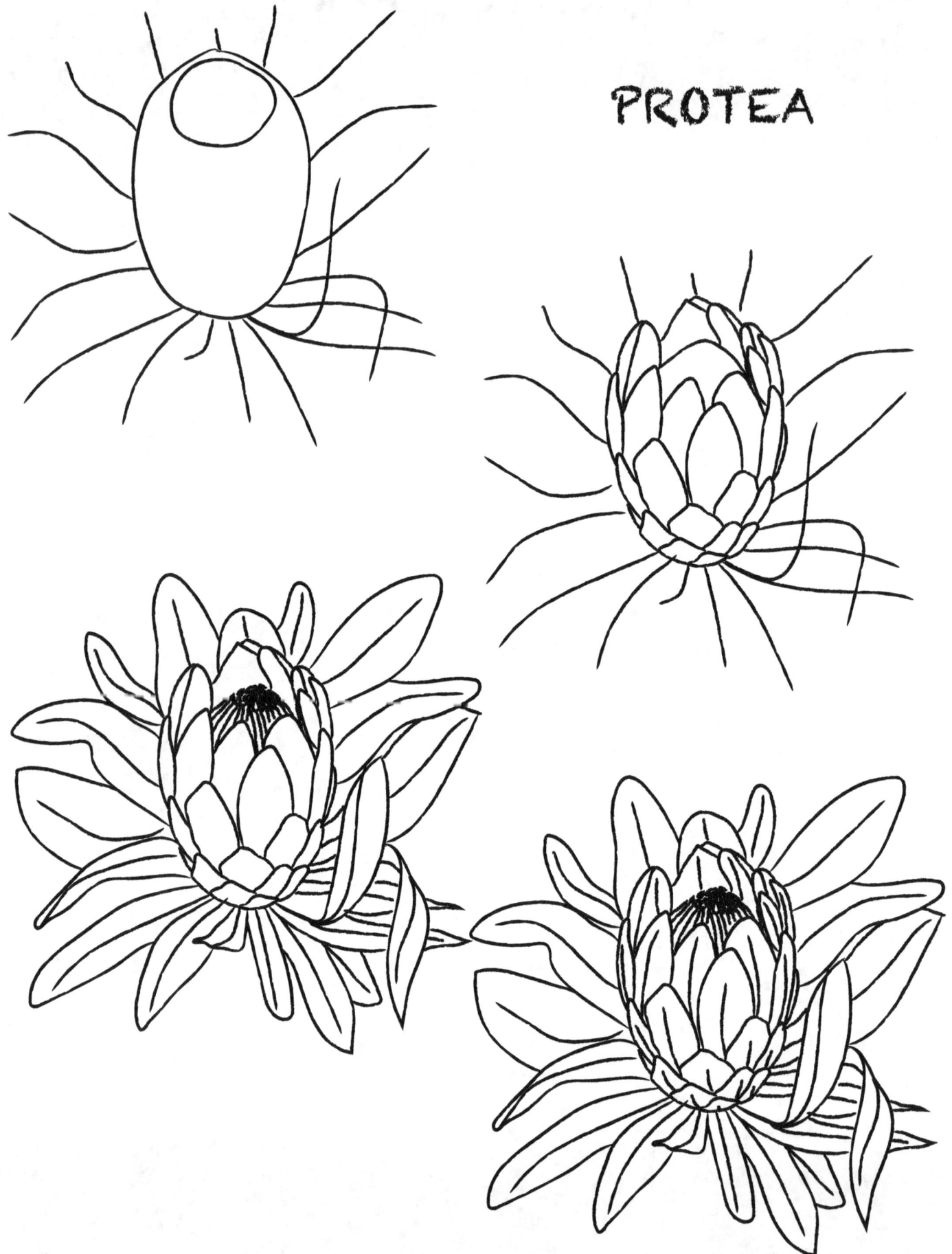

PROTEA

PRACTICE HERE!

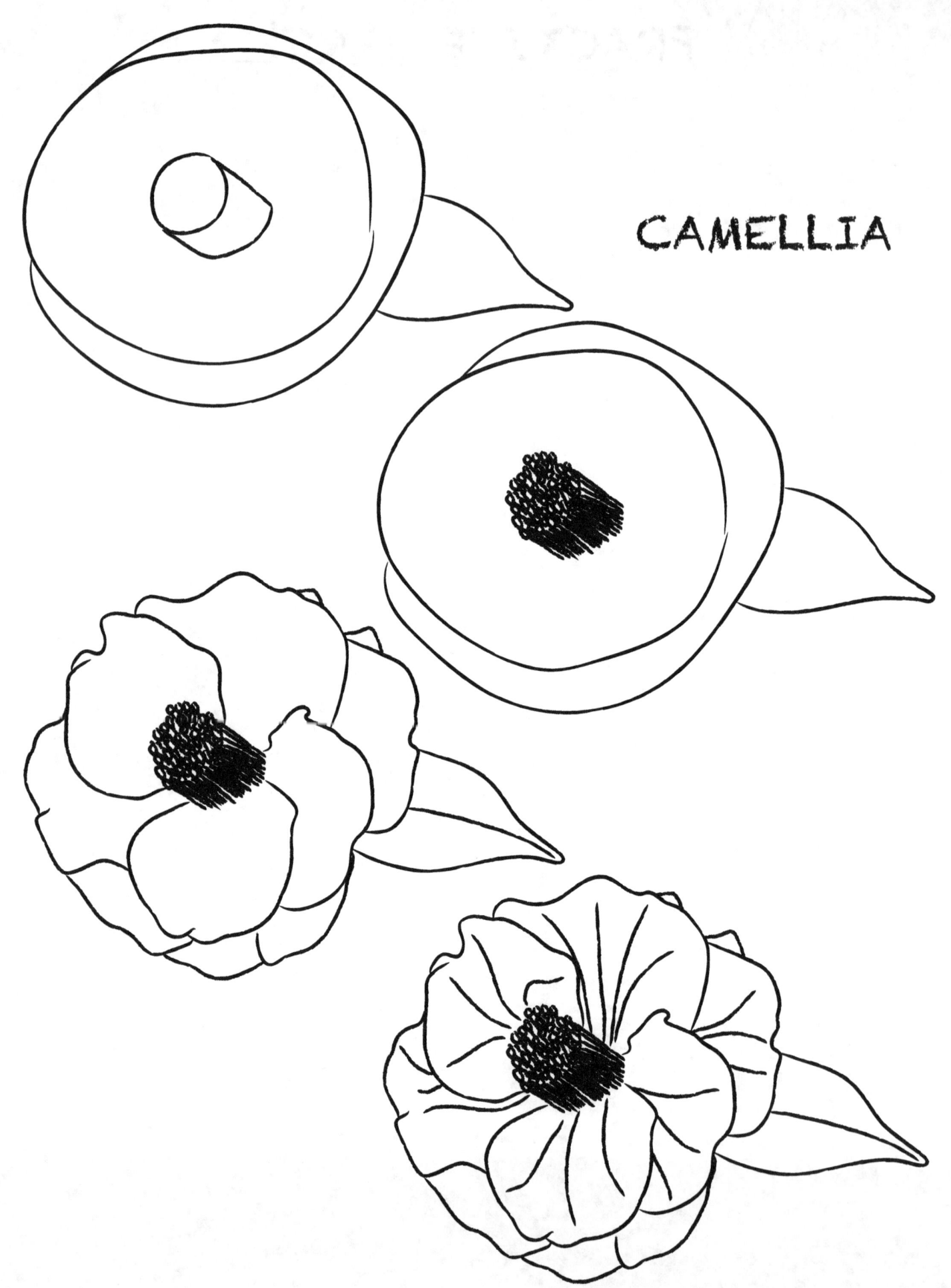

CAMELLIA

PRACTICE HERE!

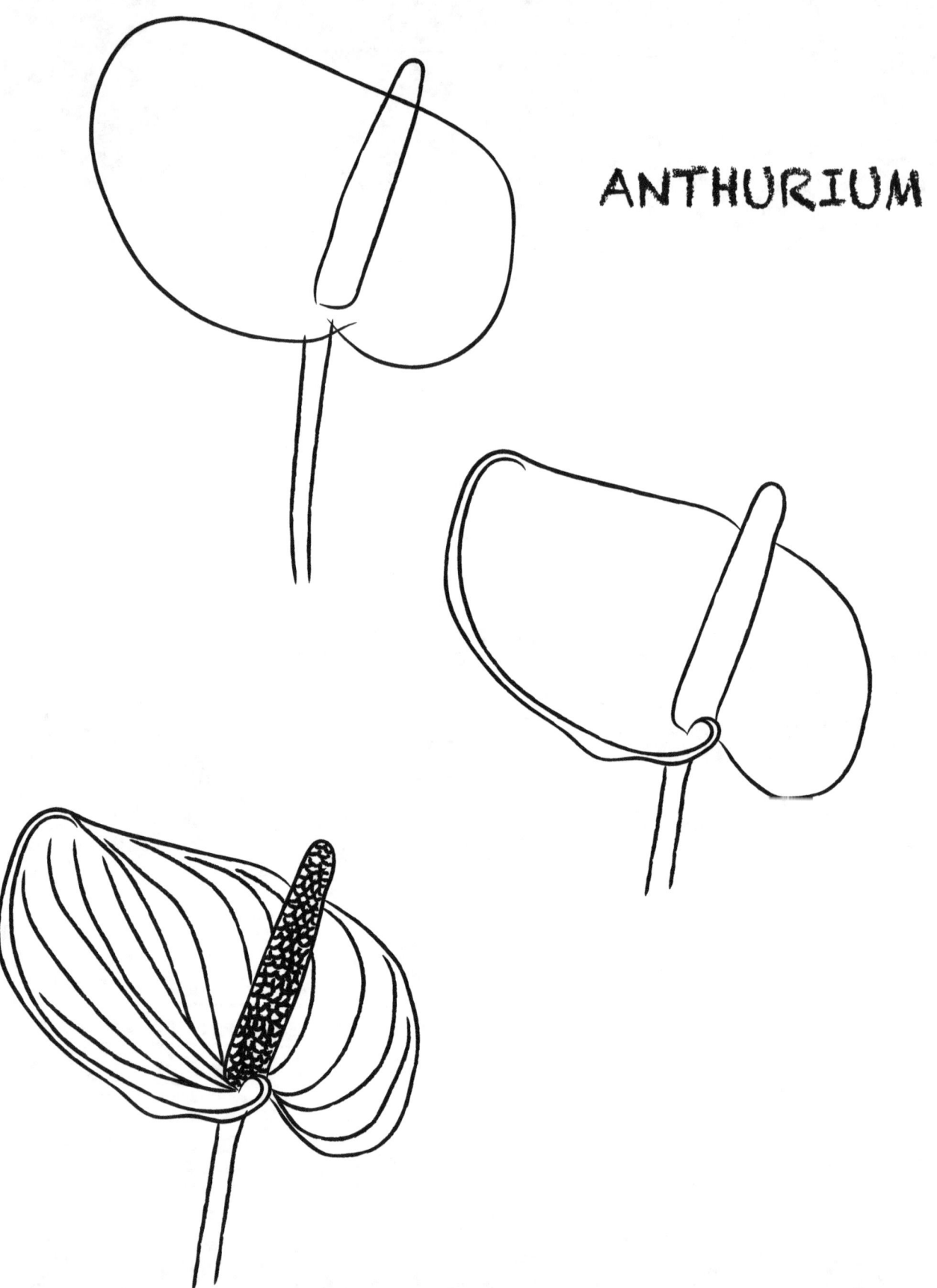

ANTHURIUM

PRACTICE HERE!

CROCUS

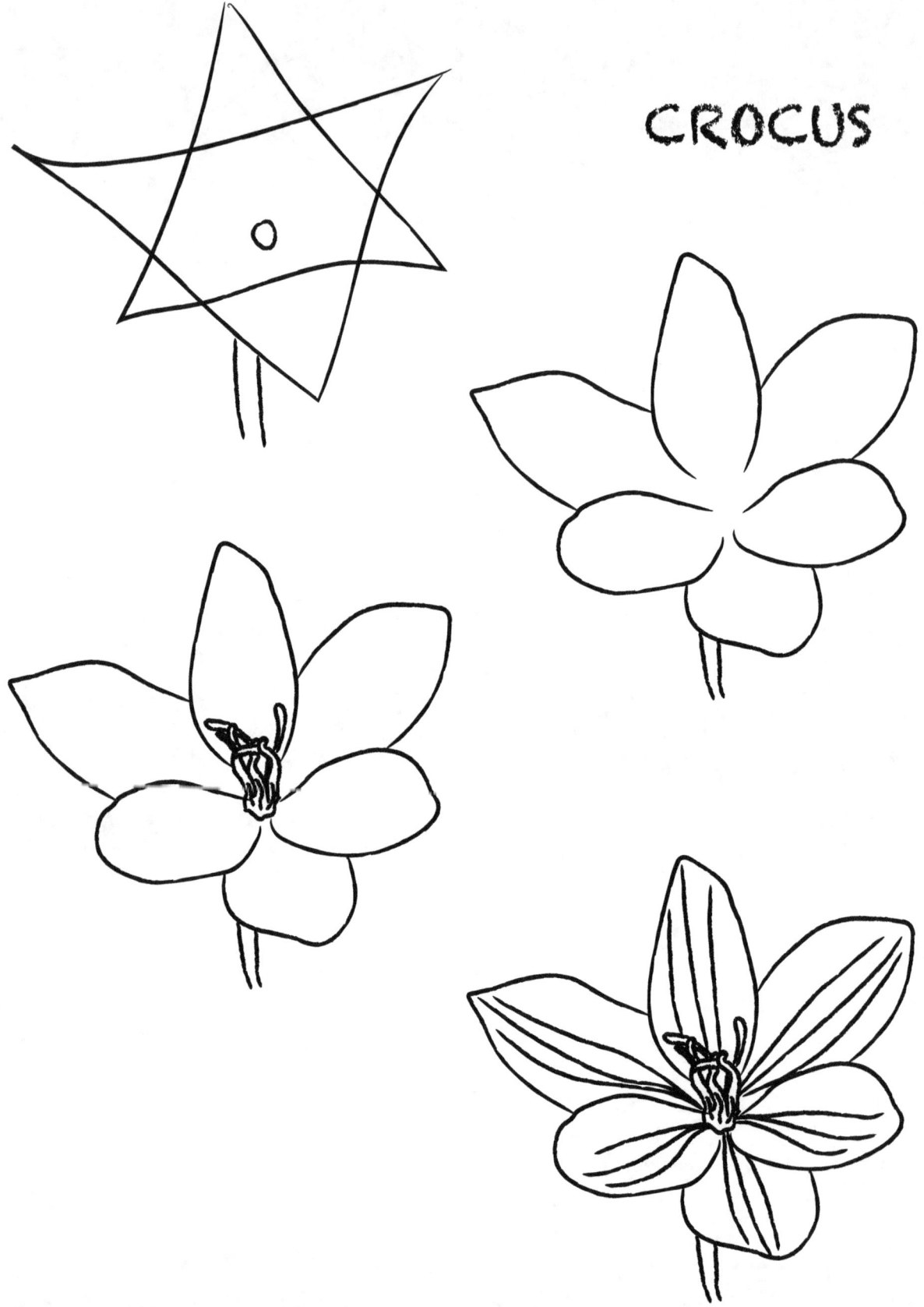

PRACTICE HERE!

PANSY

PRACTICE HERE!

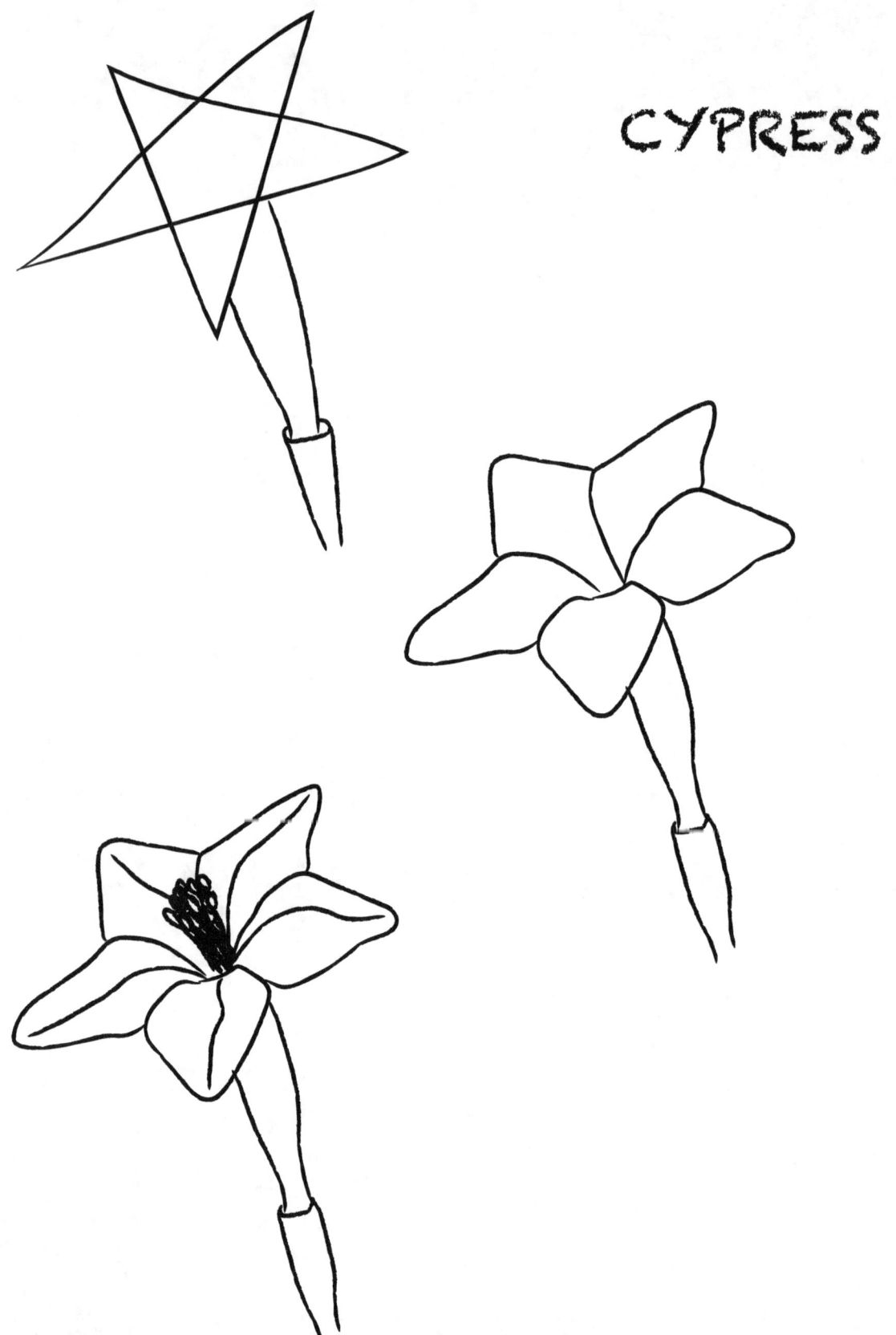

CYPRESS

PRACTICE HERE!

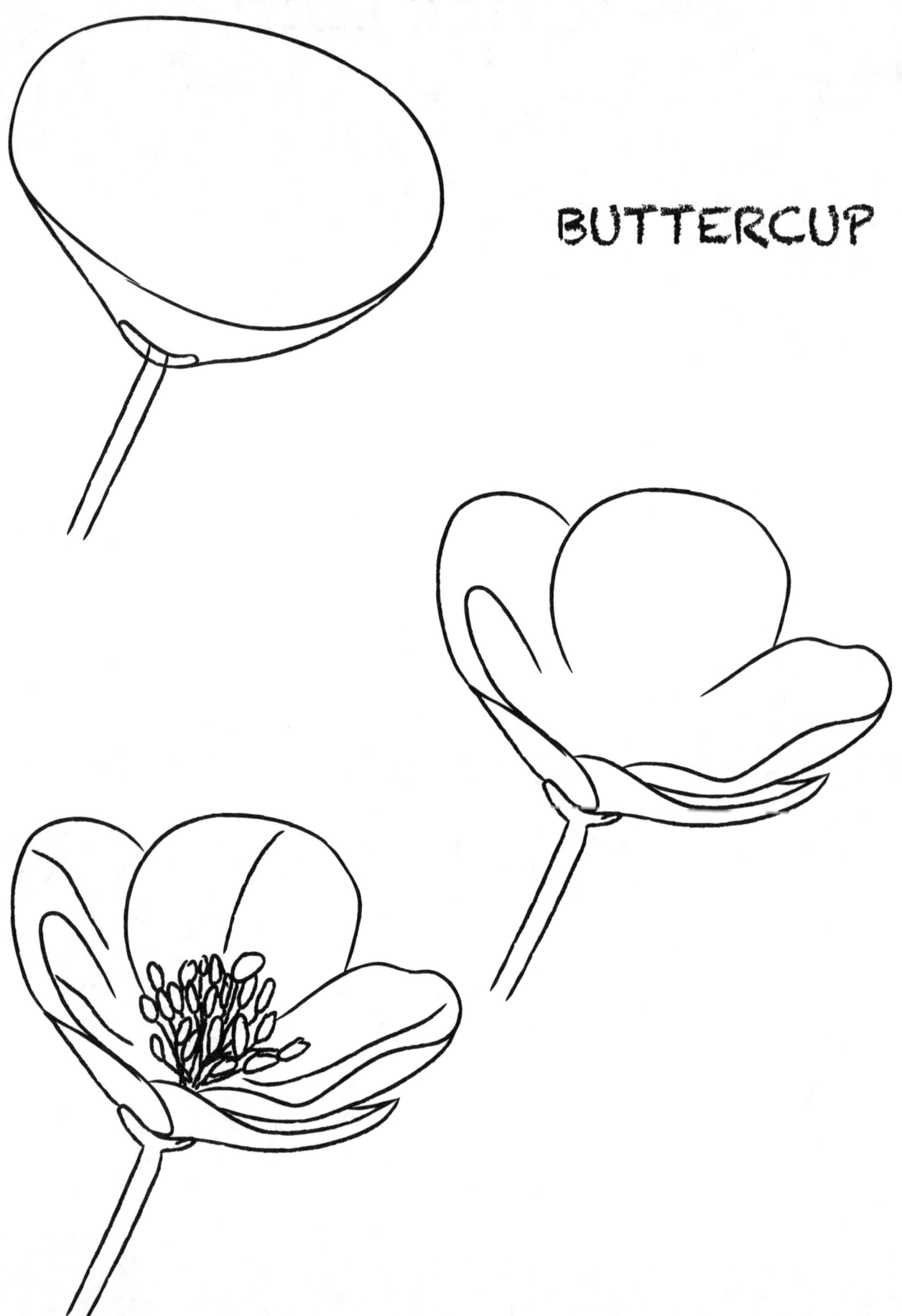

BUTTERCUP

PRACTICE HERE!

PERTUNIA

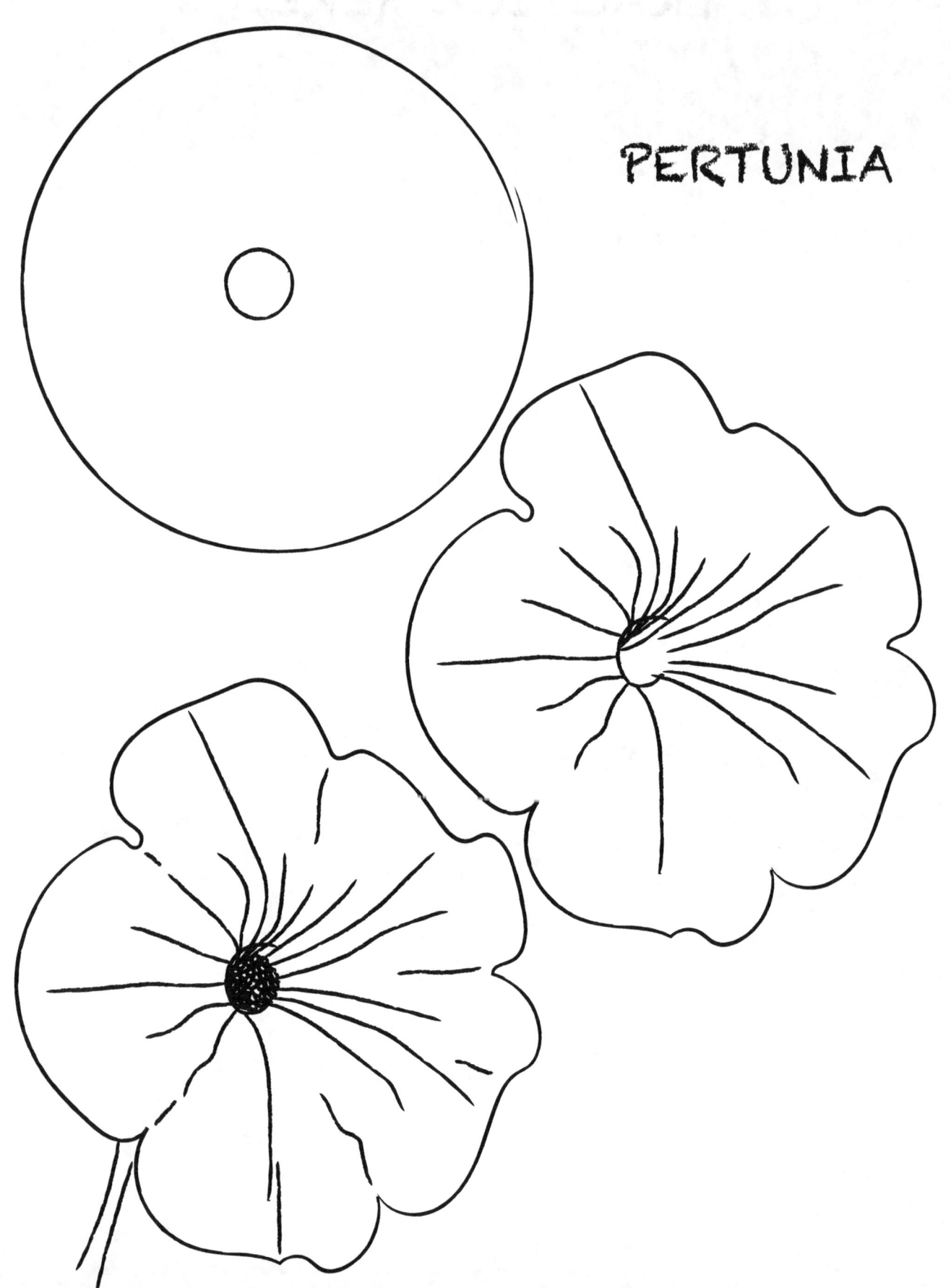

PRACTICE HERE!

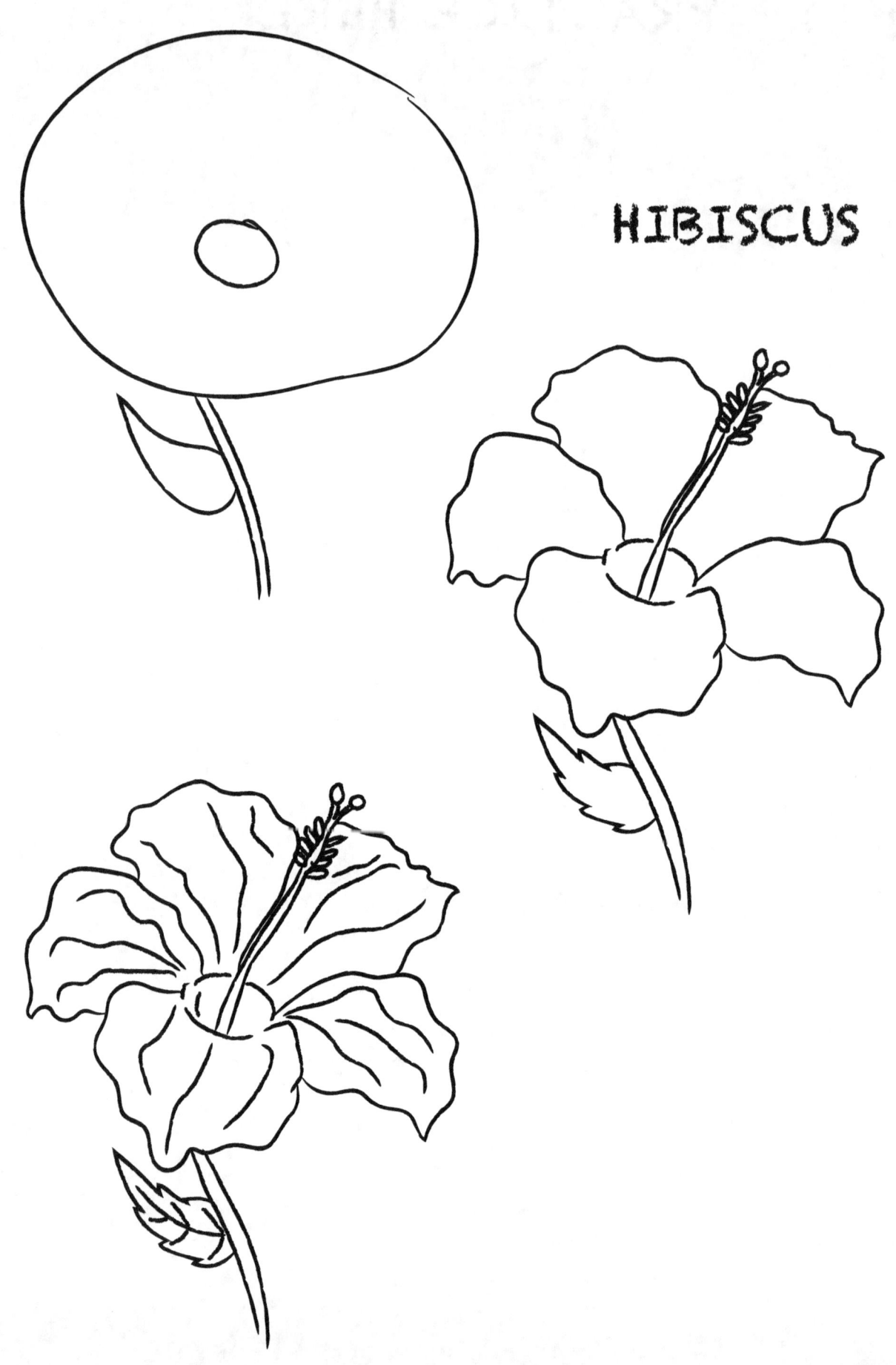

HIBISCUS

PRACTICE HERE!

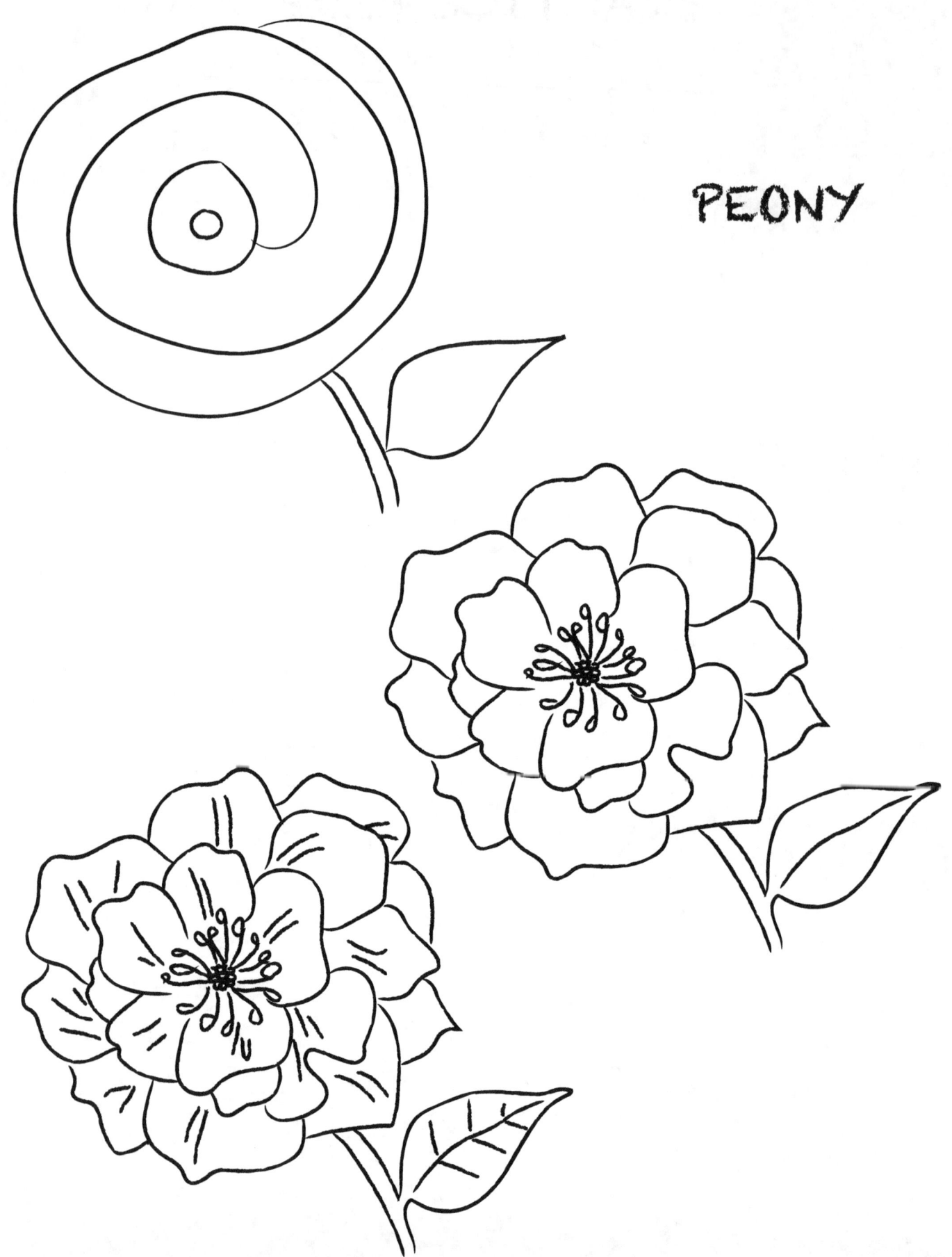

PEONY

PRACTICE HERE!

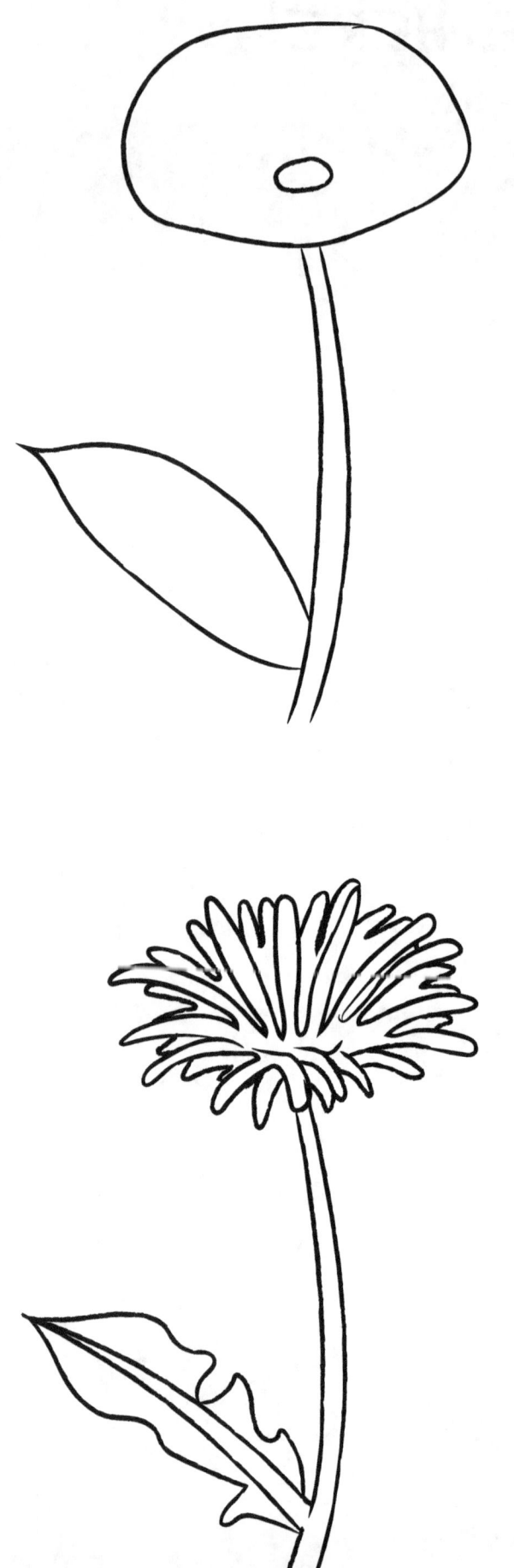
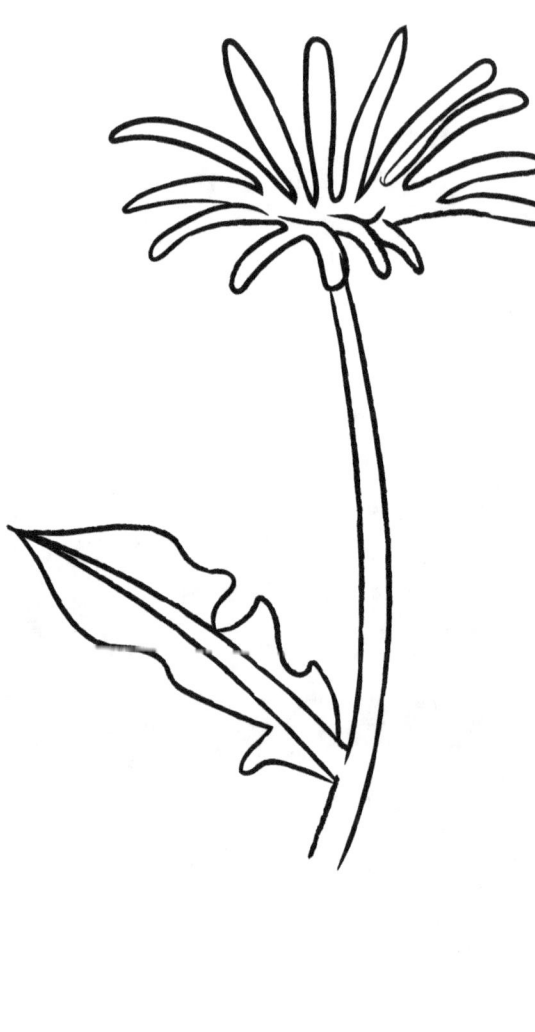

DANDELION

PRACTICE HERE!

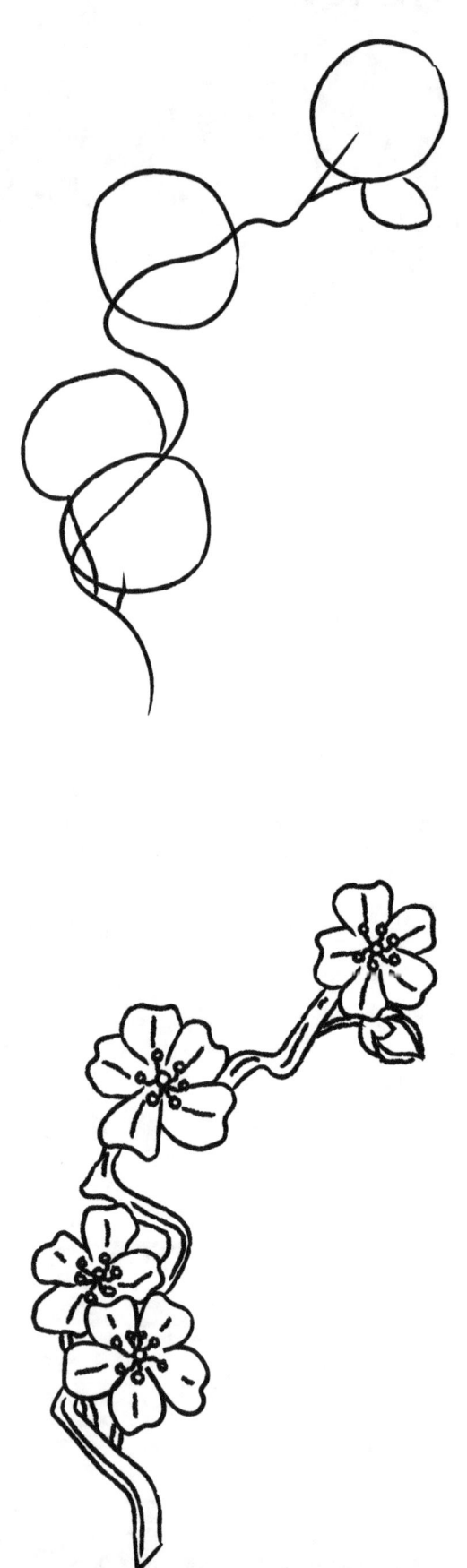
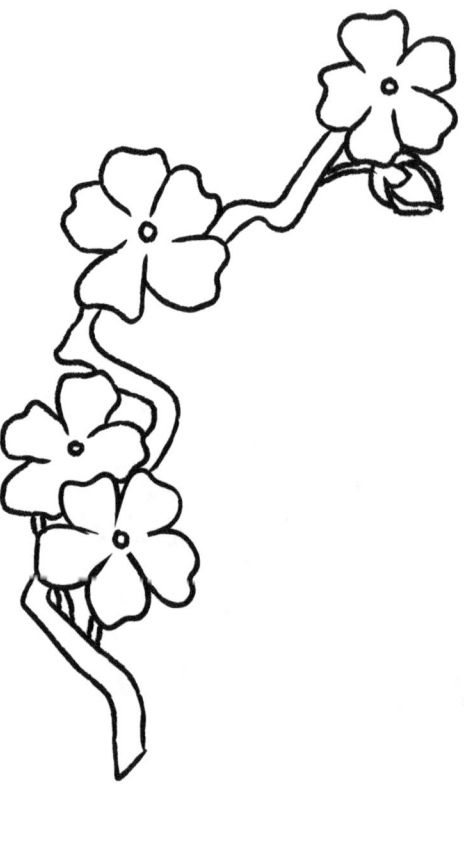

CHERRY
BLOSSOM

PRACTICE HERE!

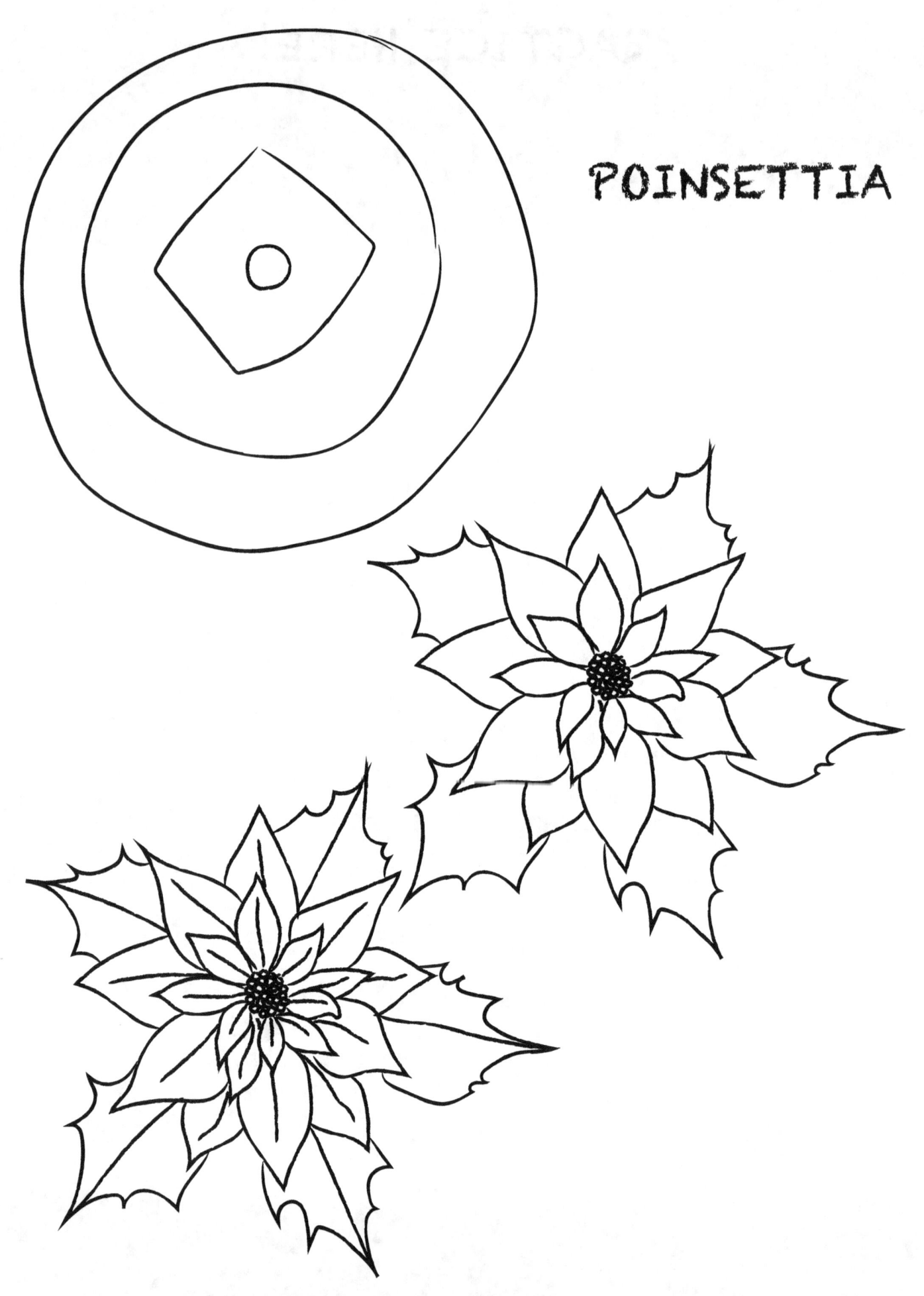

POINSETTIA

PRACTICE HERE!

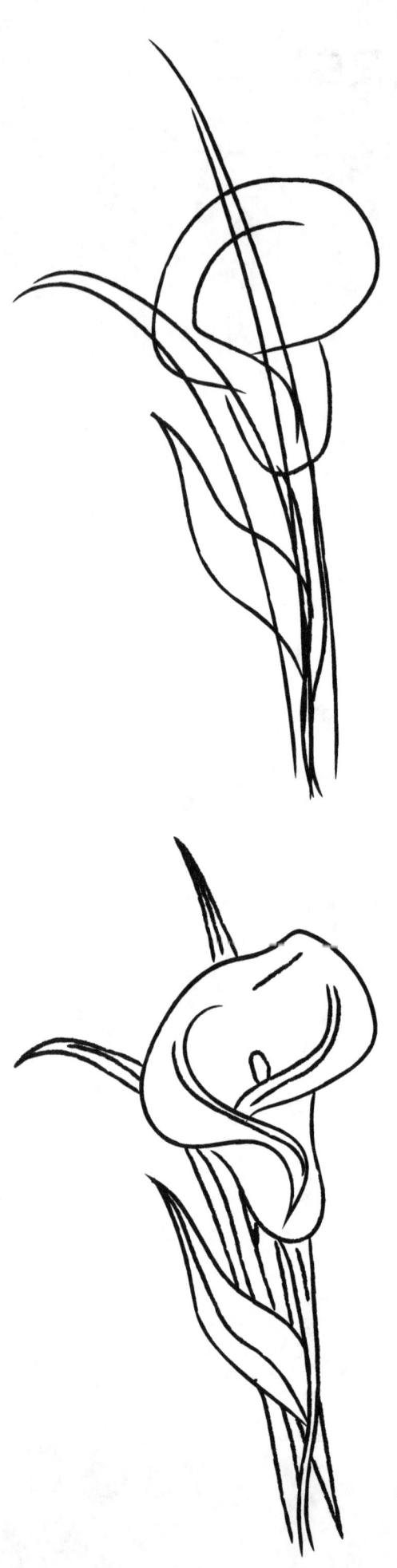
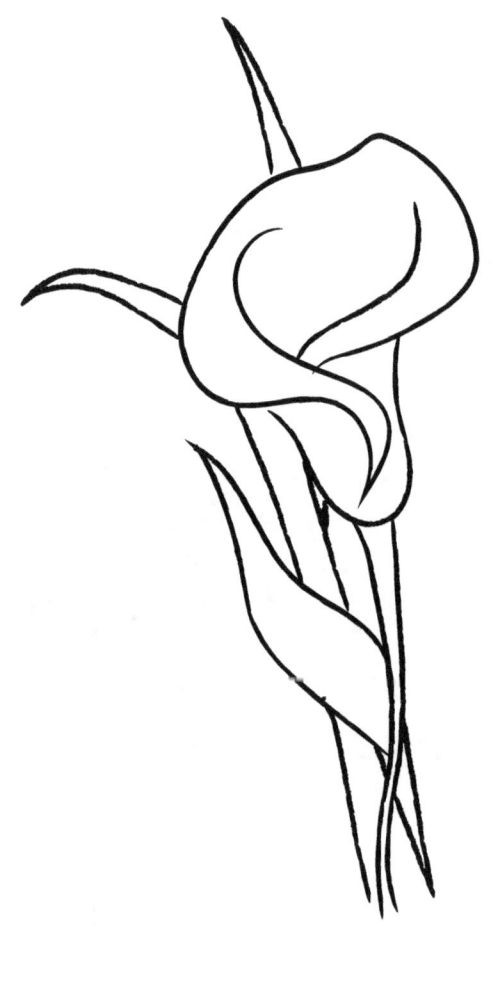

CALLALILY

PRACTICE HERE!

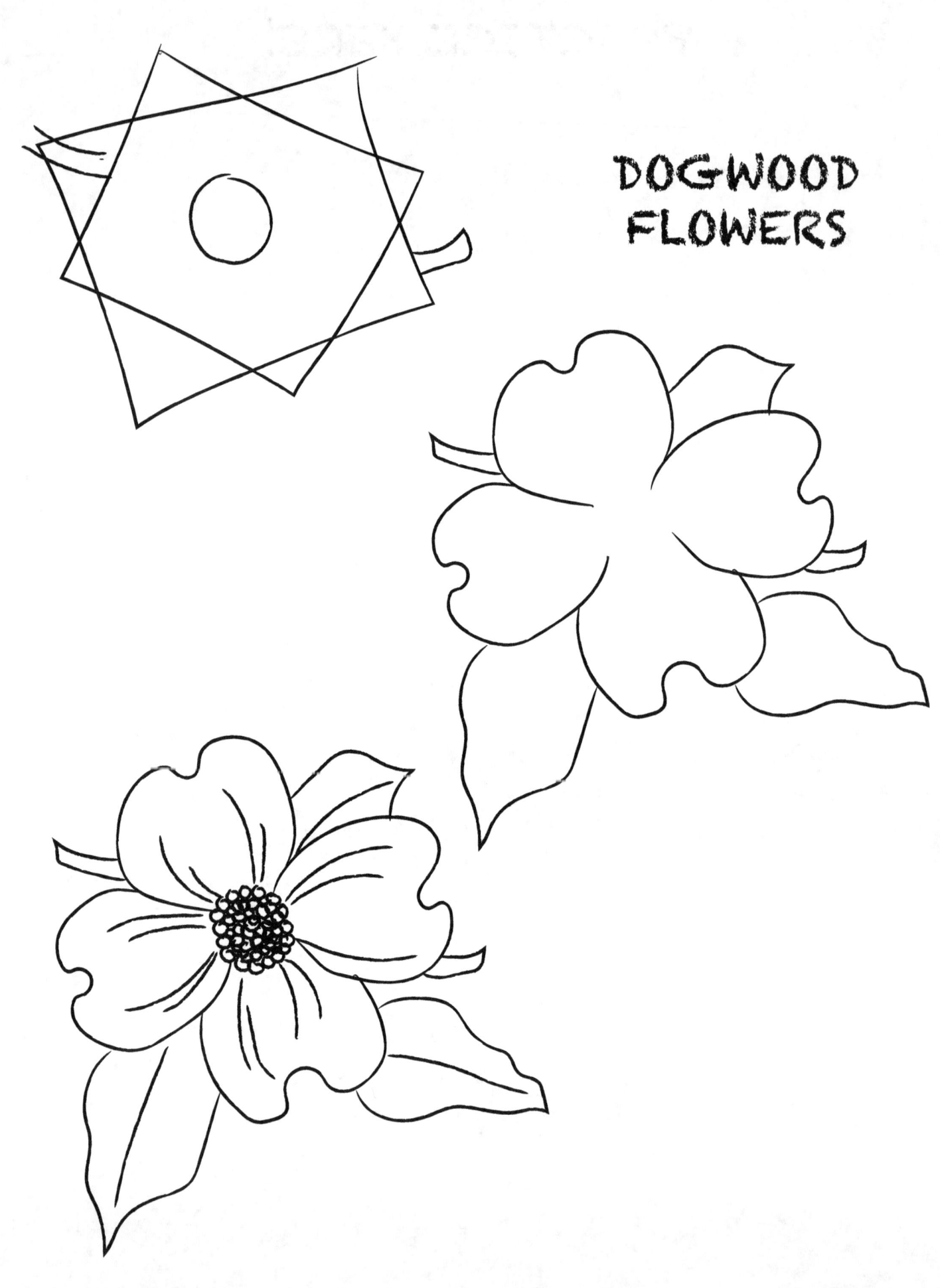

DOGWOOD
FLOWERS

PRACTICE HERE!

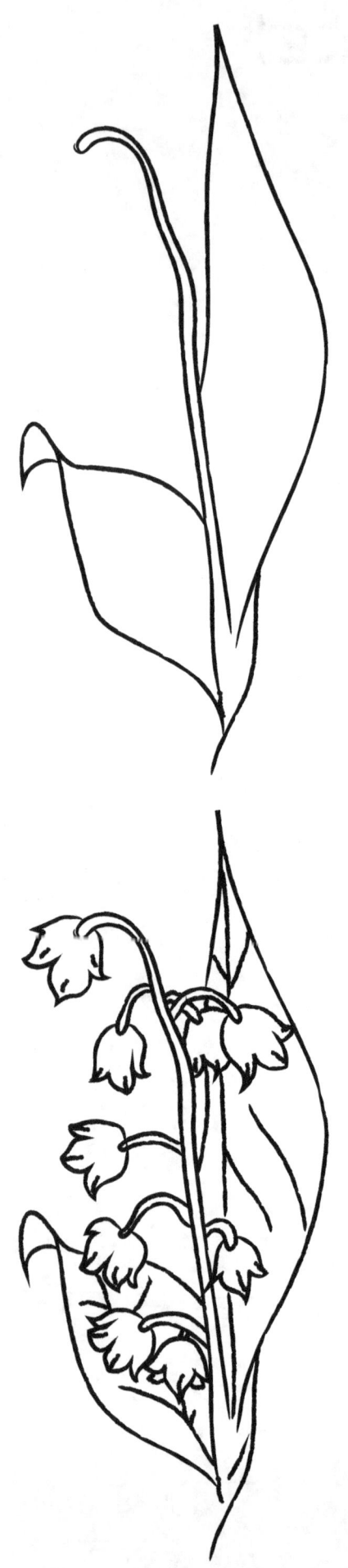
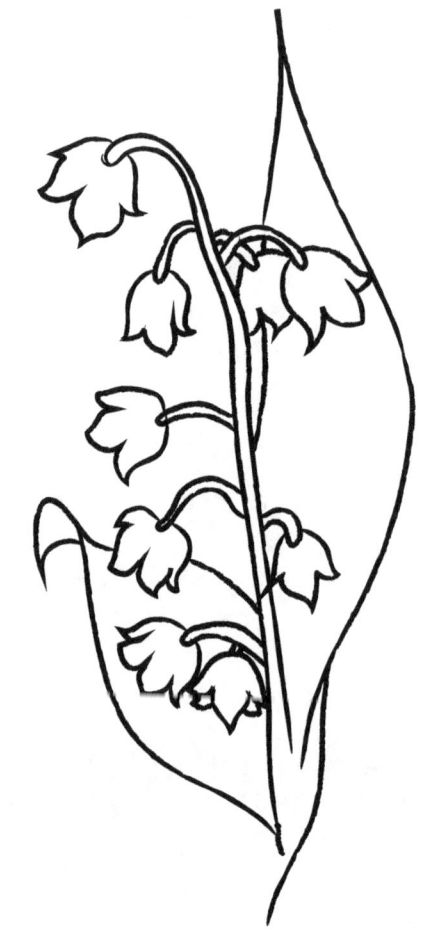

LILY OF THE
VALLEY

PRACTICE HERE!

www.ingramcontent.com/pod-product-compliance
Lightning Source LLC
Chambersburg PA
CBHW080834170526
45158CB00009B/2564